TRIBES of NATIVE AMERICA

Cahuilla

edited by Marla Felkins Ryan
and Linda Schmittroth

BLACKBIRCH®
PRESS

THOMSON
★
™
GALE

San Diego • Detroit • New York • San Francisco • Cleveland
New Haven, Conn. • Waterville, Maine • London • Munich

CAHUILLA

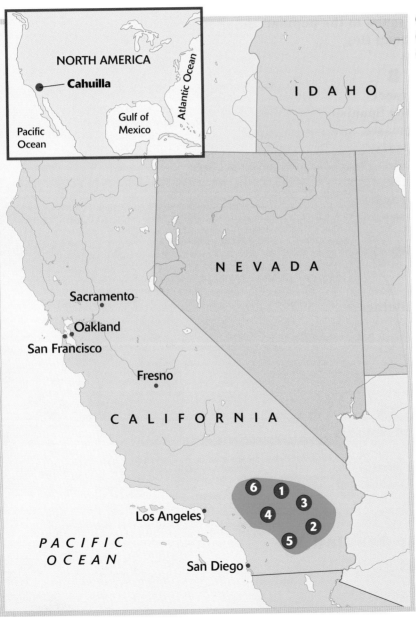

NORTH AMERICA

Cahuilla

Pacific Ocean

Gulf of Mexico

Atlantic Ocean

IDAHO

NEVADA

Sacramento

Oakland

San Francisco

Fresno

CALIFORNIA

Los Angeles

PACIFIC OCEAN

San Diego

Contemporary Communities in California

1. Agua Caliente Tribe
2. Augustine Reservation
3. Cabazon Band of Mission Indians
4. Cahuilla Reservation and Ramona Band Reservation
5. Los Coyotes Reservation
6. Morongo Reservation

Name

The name Cahuilla (pronounced *ka-WEE-ya*) comes from the word *kawiya,* which means "powerful ones."

Where are the traditional Cahuilla lands?

Members of seven bands (groups) of Cahuilla live on or near ten small reservations in southern California (see opposite page). Most live in rural areas, but part of the Agua Caliente reservation is inside the city of Palm Springs. The reservations are in the area of the tribe's traditional lands. These lands have the San Bernardino Mountains to the north, the Colorado desert to the east, and Riverside County and the Palomar Mountains to the west. Nearly two-thirds of Cahuilla lands were desert.

What has happened to the population?

There were about 6,000 Cahuilla when they first met the Spanish. By the 1850s, there were 2,500 to 3,000. In the 1970s, there were about 900. In a 1990 population count by the U.S. Bureau of the Census, people who said they were Cahuilla identified themselves this way:

Agua Caliente Cahuilla 50
Cahuilla 888
Soboba 201
Torres-Martinez 129
Other Cahuilla 26

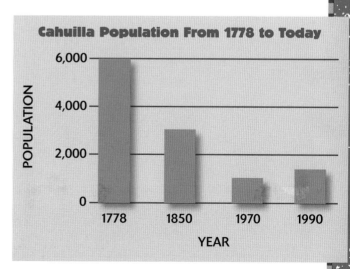

Cahuilla Population From 1778 to Today

Origins and group ties

Hundreds of years ago, there were three groups of Cahuilla from separate regions. These groups were the Palm Springs, Pass, and Desert Cahuilla. Today, the three groups are mixed on different reservations. The Cahuilla are sometimes called Mission Indians. They and other tribes lived near San Diego when the Spanish began to build Catholic missions there in the eighteenth century. The Cahuilla, though, had less contact with the missions than the other tribes did.

The Colorado Desert forms the eastern border of traditional Cahuilla lands.

The Agua Caliente band of Cahuilla lived in the desert near present-day Palm Springs. Their surroundings were rocky and dry.

The Cahuilla lived in a place where the weather could be extreme. There might be heavy rains one year and drought the next. Earthquakes and fires could strike at any time. The Cahuilla learned to live in their environment in all its moods. They were a friendly and generous people, who would give away what they owned. They were sure that if they were in need, their kindness would be repaid. Today, they live on reservations near their old homeland. They have adapted to their new lives but still hold on to some of their customs.

HISTORY

Move to the desert

Archaeologists, who study ancient cultures, say the Cahuilla first came from the parts of present-day Nevada and Colorado called the Great Basin. The Cahuilla still sing what they call "bird songs." These songs tell of their creation and their move to southern California 2,000 to 3,000 years ago. The Cahuilla found beauty in a land that many would see as harsh and barren.

This mural shows some of the daily activities of the Cahuilla Indians in their desert village.

The Cahuilla had little contact at first with the Spanish who took control of California in the late eighteenth century. The Cahuilla first met Europeans in 1774. A group of Spaniards passed through Cahuilla lands in search of a route from Mexico to the Monterey Peninsula.

Cahuilla bands guarded their land closely, especially the vital water sources. They did not want the Spanish on their lands, and fired at them with bows and arrows. When other tribes were also hostile, the Spanish gave up their search. The Cahuilla had no more contact with them for a time. Still they heard tales from other Indians. They heard stories of how badly the Spanish treated Mission Indians. But they also heard about Spanish goods and were very interested in them.

Contact with the Spanish

In the early 1800s, the Cahuilla began to visit some of the Spanish missions near the coast. There, they learned Spanish, began to wear European clothing, and learned modern skills such as ironworking. Sometimes, they were forced to work for the missions and were treated harshly by those in charge. Ever so, the Cahuilla managed to keep most of their independence while they made use of European goods.

1861
American Civil War begins

1863
Smallpox epidemic strikes Cahuilla

1865
Civil War ends

1869
Transcontinential Railroad is completed

1891
Act for Relief of Mission Indians set up Cahuilla reservations.

1917–1918
WWI fought in Europe

1929
Stock market crash begins the Great Depression

1934
Indian Reorganization Act gives back some independence to Cahuilla

1941
Bombing at Pearl Harbor forces United States into WWII

1945
WWII ends

1950s
Reservations no longer controlled by federal government

In the 1800s, Spanish priests built missions in Southern California. The Cahuilla visited some of these missions.

In 1822, Mexico took the mission lands away from Spain in the Mexican Revolution. Again the Cahuilla stayed fairly independent. They took jobs as skilled workers on cattle ranches owned by Mexicans. Their lives changed when the United States took control of California in 1848, and the California gold rush began the next year. New settlers trespassed on Cahuilla land and water sources. Tensions grew between the Cahuilla and whites.

Gold fever, diseases, and reservations

Miners and settlers brought new diseases. The Cahuilla were not immune to them. In 1863, smallpox cut down the number of Cahuilla to about 2,500. Whites took over Cahuilla water sources, and crops suffered. Then the settlers pressured the U.S. government to make reservations for the Cahuilla and other tribes. Weakened by disease, the tribes had no choice but to go to the reservations. Even then, they often lost their lands to white settlers.

In 1849, people flooded the West looking for gold.

In the next decades, the Cahuilla came to resent how the federal government tried to control their lives and take more and more of their lands. The 1891 Act for the Relief of Mission Indians took still more of the Cahuilla's land. Government schools and American missionaries tried to put an end to the Cahuilla religion, language, and political systems.

New independence

The Cahuilla tried to keep whites out of their affairs. In 1934, they won back some of their independence when the Indian Reorganization Act (IRA) was passed.

White settlers built homes in California in the 1800s. They asked the U.S. government to move the Cahuilla and other tribes onto reservations.

Members of the Paiute, Pechanga, and Cahuilla tribes met with California representative Harry Shepard in 1937 to discuss Native American concerns.

This law encouraged Native Americans to form new tribal governments. In the 1950s, the federal government no longer oversaw the reservations. This gave the Cahuilla more control over their own health, education, and welfare. In the 1960s, they got funds that helped them manage their own affairs.

Religion

The Cahuilla believed that the world is run by an unpredictable creative force. In their customs, that creative force is said to have made the first two human beings, Makat and Tamaioit, who were huge and powerful. Makat and Tamaioit then made everything else. But the creatures that came after the first two did not have the same strong powers.

Shamans (pronounced *SHAH-munz* or *SHAY-munz*), controlled rain, made food, and held ceremonies. At these ceremonies, they ate hot coals and did other amazing feats. Shamans told tales of creation in songs and dances. Music was supplied by special rattles made from gourds.

The Cahuilla believed in life after death. They thought that the dead were reborn. The dead lived a life much like the one they had left behind. But in the new life, only good things happened.

After the Cahuilla moved to reservations, missionaries tried once more to convert them. In time, many Cahuilla joined the Catholic faith. Others became Protestants. Today, Cahuilla still use parts of their own beliefs and customs.

Government

The Cahuilla lived in about a dozen villages. Each one had its own name, land, and a male ancestor common to all those in the village. Each village had

CAHUILLA WORDS

Only a few Cahuilla (about 50 in 1991) can now speak their language. Many still use some Cahuilla words, though, such as terms for relatives. For example, *qa?* means "father's father," and *qwa?* means "mother's father." (In written Cahuilla, a ? represents a sound like a gulp.) Some places have Cahuilla language classes. Cahuilla speakers such as Katherine Saubel, a respected elder and political leader, have kept the Cahuilla language alive.

A medicine man stirs a pot of medicine as he makes music with his gourd rattle.

an official called a *net,* who settled minor disputes. The net also chose areas to hunt and gather food. He represented the group at meetings of different tribes.

The net got help from a *paxaa?,* who made sure people behaved properly. He oversaw rituals and ceremonies. He led hunting parties, and told everyone about the decisions of the net.

Cahuilla leaders were usually male, but today women are active in tribal politics. Each reservation has an elected five-member business committee. The committee can make decisions without a full vote of the community.

Economy

The Cahuilla economy was a complex system of hunting and gathering. The people had a deep knowledge of local plants and animals. The people traded plants with other tribes for gourd rattles and baskets.

The Spanish brought cattle to the region in the 1800s. The cattle ate many plants. This meant there was less food for game animals and people. Some Cahuilla were unable to hunt and gather as before. They went to work on farms and ranches owned by the Spanish and other whites.

After the move to the reservations in the late 1800s, Cahuilla women made and sold woven baskets to earn money. This art is not as widely practiced

Cahuilla women
wove baskets
and sold them
to earn money.

today. Some reservations now have their own ways
to make money to help the tribe, such as bingo,
campgrounds, and gambling casinos. Though many
Cahuilla are poor, they stay on the reservations.
They want to be close to their families and they like
the fresh air and wide-open spaces.

DAILY LIFE

Families

Cahuilla children are born into the clan (group of related families) of their fathers: either the Wildcat or Coyote clan. According to writers Lowell Bean and Lisa Bourgeault: "[A] typical Cahuilla community consisted of elderly men who were brothers, their wives, and their sons and nephews, together with their wives and children. All of these related people worked and played together."

Cahuilla children are born into one of two clans.

Education

Children began to learn their adult roles when they were toddlers, as they watched adults and played. Boys played games that taught coordination and made their muscles strong (like footraces and kickball). These games helped them become quick, expert hunters. Girls learned skills they would need to weave baskets and gather small seeds. Children learned their history and religion from stories handed down from past generations. Elders won respect for all that they knew about the tribe's history. They also told young people what to do when natural disasters took place.

Today, Cahuilla children go to public schools, colleges, and trade schools. Some reservations also hold classes in native language and culture.

A Cahuilla family poses outside their house in the Palm Desert.

Homes and buildings

Cahuilla homes depended on where the people lived. Some families put brush shelters over the fronts of caves. Some built cone-shaped homes of cedar bark. The Cahuilla used Y-shaped supports and thatched roofs and walls. Sometimes they plastered the walls. Many of their homes were dome-shaped, but some were rectangular.

At the center of the village was the largest building, the ceremonial house. The *net* lived in or near it. The house usually had a small area where sacred items were kept, and a large place for religious dances. Outside was a smaller dance area. Attached to the house was a place to cook food for ceremonies. Nearby were granaries—large nest-like baskets used to store food—and a sweathouse. Men would go to the sweat-house for social and ritual sweatbaths, and to discuss important matters.

Some Cahuilla homes are built with thatched roofs and walls.

Cahuilla families often built their homes close together. Some tribes had winter and summer villages, but the Cahuilla used the same villages all year round. These villages were near water and food sources. Many were in or near canyons that could shield them from harsh winds. The people marked the boundaries of their lands with designs carved into rocks. Cahuilla homes today tend to be more spread out, on plots of land large enough to farm or have cattle ranches.

Food

The Cahuilla diet was well rounded and nutritious. The people hunted, harvested, and grew their foods.

Large nest-shaped baskets held stored grain.

The men hunted, the women picked plants and seeds, and children and older people cooked.

The Cahuilla knew when hundreds of kinds of plants would be ripe. They even pruned and watered crops they had not planted, such as pine nuts, cactus, and mesquite (pronounced *meh-SKEET*) beans. Pine nuts were roasted on coals in shallow trays or baskets. Cactus was boiled or eaten fresh, and mesquite beans were dried and pounded into a fine meal.

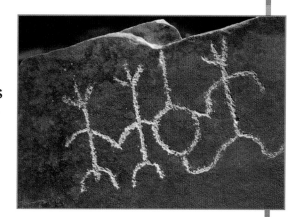

The Cahuilla carved pictures into the rocks that surrounded their villages.

The Cahuilla harvested and roasted pinenuts, which grew naturally in the desert.

Acorns were ground into flour, then covered with boiling water.

Acorns were a big part of the diet. They were ground into a flour and then covered with boiling water to take out the poisonous tannic acid. The Cahuilla also planted corn, beans, melons, and squash.

The Cahuilla today eat many traditional foods. They still enjoy acorns and cactus buds, and they also eat deer and quail. They can no longer hunt mountain sheep and antelope, though, which were once highly valued for their tasty meat.

Clothing

Many years ago, the Cahuilla wore clothes made of the natural materials they could find. They pounded mesquite bark into a soft material for women's skirts and babies' diapers. They also used mesquite bark for sandals, and made blankets out of strips of rabbit fur. Men wore deerskin and sheepskin breech-cloths (garments with front and back flaps that hung from the waist). Body paint was used for ceremonies, and facial tattoos were common.

After they met the Spanish in the late eighteenth century, many Cahuilla began to wear European-style clothing. They mixed pants, shirts, skirts, and jackets with traditional clothing.

Bark from mesquite trees was used to make the Cahuilla's clothing.

Healing

The Cahuilla believed that when the spirits were displeased, they made people sick. Shamans were then called. To heal, they sometimes sucked on the affected part of the patient's body to take out the ailment. Other times, they blew, spit on, stroked, or rubbed the area. Herbs were used, or a pit was dug and warmed with hot rocks for the sick person to lie in. Those who lived near what is now Palm Springs used the hot springs there as a cure for illness.

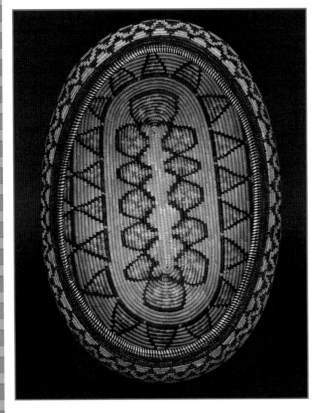

The Cahuilla used different colored grass to create beautiful baskets.

Arts

Once they had learned to live in the desert, Cahuilla people had time to make crafts. Men made heavy baskets that could be used to hold plants and seeds. Women made beautiful coiled baskets from grasses and rushes of varied colors. The baskets were decorated with designs of rattlesnakes, turtles, stars, and eagles. To give gifts was part of all Cahuilla ceremonies, and often the gifts were baskets or items given in baskets.

CUSTOMS

Ceremonies and festivals

The Cahuilla had a special way to deal with death. When a person died, his or her home and belongings were burned. This was believed to set the spirit free to enjoy the belongings in the next world. The Cahuilla's most important ritual was a yearly ceremony to mourn the dead. This custom continues today with a Memorial Day fiesta. This event celebrates Cahuilla culture and honors Cahuilla men who died in service during World War II (1939–1945).

The Cahuilla also have other rituals, such as the eagle ceremony. For this, they form a large circle outside the ceremonial house. In the middle of the circle, a dancer moves like an eagle and hits two sticks together to help the other people sing. The dancer wears an eagle feather headdress and skirt. The ceremonial house is still a center for culture and community, even for Cahuilla people who do not live and work on the reservation.

The Cahuilla set fire to a dead person's possessions to free the deceased's spirit.

Marriage

To know one's ancestors was very important, because the Cahuilla would not marry anyone even remotely related to

ORIGIN OF THE BIRDS

Two of the main figures in Cahuilla tales are Mukat and his brother Tamaioit. They are the first two beings from whom all other creatures came. This story, "Origin of the Birds," was told by a man named Alexandro of Morongo. He told it to anthropologist Lucile Hooper in 1918 (anthropologists study human cultures). Hooper claimed that Alexandro gave her a short

Cahuilla creation stories about pelicans and other birds have been told for many generations.

version of the tale, because it would have taken all night to name the birds.

When Mukat died, the people who were still living at the big house did not know where to go or what to do. They went east, west, north, south, above, and below. They could not decide which direction they were intended to take. They finally reached the edge of the water and here they saw Sovalivil (pelican). He told them how to find Tamaioit. When they found him, he asked why they came to him. "I am different from all of you, he said, so I cannot help you, I fear. There is one thing I might suggest, however. I created the willow tree, which I forgot to bring with me; get the branches of that and brush yourselves with it and perhaps you will then know what to do." So they all returned and brushed themselves with the willow, then started out once more. A few, who became tired, stopped, and turned themselves into rocks and trees. The others reached the top of Mount San Jacinto and here they slept that night. At dawn, Isel (a bird with a yellow breast that is often seen around swamps), awoke them and made them look around. A bird which is larger than a buzzard told them not to look, that there was nothing to see. Nevertheless, they all looked around and saw many beautiful green fields. They decided to go to these. On the way, one by one, they stopped. These that stopped became birds. When the others returned that way, they named the birds.

SOURCE: Lucile Hooper. "The Cahuilla Indians." University of California Publications in Archaeology and Ethnology, 16 (April 10, 1920).

Marriages are arranged in traditional Cahuilla culture. The parents of the groom choose a bride from another Cahuilla clan.

them. A boy's parents carefully chose a bride from another clan. The boy's father then offered the girl's father a gift. If he took the gift, his daughter moved into the home of the boy's family. There was no further ceremony.

Current tribal issues

The Cahuilla work hard to hold on to their culture. A big part of this effort can be seen at the Malki Museum on the Morongo Reservation. Cahuilla scholars and storytellers teach others about Cahuilla culture and history.

The Cahuilla are active in political issues such as land and water conservation. Outside developers, oil companies, and highway builders want to use Cahuilla lands. The Cahuilla want to prevent this from happening.

A tribal leader stands outside a Cahuilla ceremonial house.

In December 2000, California representative Mary Bono (lower left) spoke at a ceremony to honor a new national monument. The Agua Caliente Cahuilla helped establish the monument.

Notable people

Ruby Modesto (1913-1980) spoke Cahuilla as a child. She knew a great deal about her culture. Modesto became a medicine woman when she was in her forties. In her book *Not for Innocent Ears,* she described how it became her job to heal people.

Political leader Juan Antonio (born c. 1783) fought in the 1840s and 1850s to keep Cahuilla lands out of the hands of Mexican and American settlers.

For Further Reading

Bean, Lowell John, and Lisa Bourgeault. *The Cahuilla.* New York: Chelsea House Publishers, 1989.

Jackson, Helen Hunt. *Ramona.* New York: Signet, 1988.

Milanovich, Richard, "Beauty in the Desert," in *All Roads Are Good: Native Voices on Life and Culture.* Washington, D.C.: Smithsonian Institution, 1994.

Modesto, Ruby. *Not for Innocent Ears: Spiritual Traditions of a Cahuilla Medicine Woman.* Cottonwood, CA: Sweetlight Books, 1989.

Saubel, Katherine. *I'isniyatami (designs): A Cahuilla Word Book.* Banning, CA: Malki Museum Press, 1977.

Glossary

Adapt to adjust to a new situation

Archaeologist a person who studies past human life and activities

Basin a large or small depression in the surface of the land or in the ocean floor

Conservation a careful preservation and protection of something

Drought a period of dryness, especially when prolonged, that causes extensive damage to crops or prevents their successful growth

Environment the conditions by which one is surrounded

Immune protected against

Mesquite trees found in the southwestern United States

Mission a local church or parish dependent on a larger religious organization for direction or financial support

Peninsula a piece of land jutting out into the water

Reservation land set aside and given to Native Americans

Rural relating to the country, country people or life, or agriculture

Shaman a priest or priestess who uses magic for the purpose of curing the sick, divining the hidden, and controlling events

Thatched covered

Vital important

Welfare a government assistance program

Index